Happily Broken: Discovering Happiness
through Pain and Suffering

By Clementine Bihiga

1

This book is dedicated to my parents,

Philippe and Eudosie Bizimana.

When I look at both of you, I see Jesus. Thank you for being such great role models.

Agakobwa Kanyu Kitonda,
(your very timid daughter)

Clementine Bihiga.

Table of Contents

Introduction 5

Genesis of Breaking.................................7

Exodus Out of Rwanda 11

Breaking in Congo 13

Breaking in Kenya.................................24

Breaking in the United States 37

Ridiculous Happiness 58

The Best Thanksgiving! 70

Breaking into a Whole...........................74

Happily Broken.....................................80

Many Thanks to:...................................82

More on Me 83

Need a Speaker or a Workshop Leader?..............84

Satisfied Customers 88

Introduction

Most of us suffer some sort of pain at some point in our lives. Sometimes, the suffering is so unbearable that we become angry and ask, Why God? Why me? I'm not a bad person. I'm a decent person, and I try to live right. Why me? Why me?

Then we come to a realization! Jesus was perfect, yet

He was born in a manger.
He became a refugee in his infancy.
He grew up an alien in Egypt.
He grew up in a poor family.
He was misunderstood by all, including his family.
He was hungry and cursed a fig tree.
He associated with the lowly.
He depended on God through prayer.
He was betrayed and denied by His closest friends.
He was mocked and beaten.
He was subject to an unjust trial.

He suffered for doing the right thing.

He was made naked in public.

He was crucified.

He had a simple burial.

The question we should be asking ourselves when we are suffering should not be *Why me*? Instead, we should ask, *Why Not Me?* We need to embrace the suffering and breaking and believe good things are to come!

Genesis of Breaking

Breaking: *To come into being by or as if by bursting forth*

Merriam-Webster's Dictionary

Death of a President

The death of former Rwandan president Juvenal Habyarimana in 1994 is what sparked everything. My life was going to change because some man I had never met was killed. People always ask who killed Mr. Habyarimana. Knowing who killed the president would lead to finding whoever was responsible for the genocide that resulted in the death of over 800,000 Rwandans in just three months. The problem with this question is that it's political, and I'm not a politician. The wrong answer to this question can get you into trouble. All I know is that the man was dead, and I didn't do it. Let's leave it at that!

Mass Massacre

The massacre was insane. Rwandans were being butchered left and right as if living were going out of style. People who had lived together in harmony were all of a sudden killing each other with machetes, kitchen knives, hammers, and guns. Radios were going viral with hate messages encouraging people to kill each other, and they did. It's as if the devil had enveloped the whole country, and people lost their way. It's as if they were no longer human. The love that was always in the air had suddenly vanished. Everyone was looking to get out, but most people hid in their compounds for fear of going outside and being murdered.

I recall hearing a story of how one of our close family friends was killed along with his family. As the gang of killers drove in their trucks shouting hate messages and waving their machetes, our friend could hear them approaching his home. He knew it was over. He decided to take his wife and children outside to the front porch, handed each one of them a rosary, and the whole family sat at the porch while reciting the rosary and waited for the killers to arrive. When the killers got to the house, they quickly got out of the truck, chopped off each family member's head, and quickly left to go to the next house. The family died while praying.

A few weeks before my family and I left Rwanda, I was sitting on our porch inside our big compound on a beautiful, sunny morning. I hadn't slept well the night before. I had nightmares, which were constantly interrupted by chaos and screaming outside. I was happy that morning had come. I quietly stared at the ladder that lay against the compound wall. If I climbed that ladder, I would have a view of the street and be able to see for myself what had happened during all the chaos. My parents had forbidden us from climbing the ladder, but the curious eight-year-old that I was would not let me. I wanted to know what was outside the protection of the compound wall. I quickly scanned my surroundings to make sure no one was watching and decided to climb the ladder. One step at a time, I climbed with my anticipation rising the higher I got. I finally made it to the top of the ladder and FROZE!

I couldn't believe what I saw. The street was filled with blood and lifeless bodies. Some machetes that were used to butcher my fellow citizens were still on the ground. I saw the body of a neighbor. The head was in a ditch, and the rest of the body was in the street. Some of these bodies must have been there for quite some time because the stench was unbearable.Why did I go up the ladder? Why didn't I listen to my parents? How am I supposed to get this horrible image out of my head? Why is this happening? What is going on? Where is God? WHY?? These were some of the questions that were running through my mind as my tiny body trembled while slowly descending the ladder in tears. No one was to know that I went up the ladder; I would be in big trouble. I sat down in the same spot I had been sitting before I forever scarred my innocence and just stared at nothing. I felt like a zombie. My life had forever changed. The breaking had slowly begun.

Exodus Out of Rwanda

After the massacre ended in our neighborhood, the guerilla army closed in and came into our neighborhood. This was round two of killings. This time, though, the army had bombs and guns and shot anyone who got in their way. If you were alive, you were a target. People started to quickly take the few belongings they could carry and poured into the streets, running for their lives. The faster they got out of the country, the better chance they had of surviving the whole ordeal. People were on foot, and some were in cars. People were falling and stepping on one another, and some were screaming at each other out of frustration. At the time, my mother was pregnant with my little brother, the seventh sibling of the family.

We had a small compact car, and my mother and younger siblings piled into it, while my two older brothers and I walked beside them. We were trying very hard to stay together because at this point many families had lost their loved ones during the chaos. Bullets and bombs were flying and exploding all around us. People kept falling dead, and whoever didn't get hit would just keep moving forward. Two people could be holding hands, and a bullet would hit one and that person would be killed. The lucky survivor would drop the other one on the street and keep moving. There was no time to mourn or check to see if they were all right. Time was of the essence. Mourning could wait. Throughout this whole drama, I looked up and realized that our family car was not next to us anymore. My mother and younger siblings had disappeared. Had they been killed by one of the bombs? What would I do without my mother? I was eight years old, and I was lost, confused, angry, scared, and hungry. My mother wasn't around, which probably meant I needed to take care of my two older brothers. I had it cut out for me. I had to grow up fast. Playtime was over.

Breaking in Congo

We kept walking, following the crowd. We were not sure where we were going, but stopping was not an option. We needed to get out of Rwanda. It felt as though we had been walking for a month before we got to the border of Rwanda and Congo, but the walk was actually about two days. I felt such a huge relief when I finally crossed the border. I was finally free. I was in a totally different country, and no one could touch me. Without my mother around to tell us what to do next, though, my brothers and I had to rely on ourselves.

We saw a group of children our age walking quickly up the dirt road as if they knew where they were going. They were probably lost just like we were, but we decided to follow them anyway. After what seemed like hours of walking, we came upon an abandoned house and decided to stay there with a woman and her seven young boys. I was the only girl in the group. All the other children were boys, ranging from six to seventeen years old. The woman tried her best to cook and feed us all. People passing by would occasionally throw food to us, and we would all jump on it, but I was having a difficult time eating because I missed my own mother, and the boys were just too rough. We all sat in a circle around a small plate of food, and we would eat with our fingers. I would eat slowly, and my brothers would look at me and encourage me to eat faster because there wasn't enough food. Everyone had one mouthful of food, and then it would be gone. In my case, I never made it to the plate. I was malnourished and depressed.

At night, we would sleep on the bare dirt floor. I always hoped I would wake up to find that this was a nightmare, but I quickly realized that it was reality. I would sit outside by myself and cry all day. My eldest brother would come and put me on his lap and say, "Mom is coming tomorrow." Tomorrow arrived, but my mother didn't come. He would tell me the same thing the following day, but she still didn't come. My poor brother was as terrified as I was because he, too, didn't know when our mother was coming or if she would ever come at all.

One day as I sat on a big rock outside the house I saw a car approaching. Who could this be? We hardly ever saw cars come down the road. As the car came closer, it looked more and more familiar. Yes! It was my mother and younger siblings! Apparently, several radio stations were announcing the whereabouts of lost children, and that's how they located us. Thank God for the media! Tomorrow had come at last, and my mother was here, but we were not going back home to Rwanda!

Instead, we went to a town in Congo (Zaire) and rented a house. It had no bathroom, so we would wake up every morning and knock on our neighbors' doors and beg to use their restrooms. Most of them would tell us to leave their property, but some felt sorry for us. Soon thereafter, my mother gave birth to another boy, and things seemed as if they were getting as close to normal as possible. My parents had to pick two children to go to school since they couldn't afford to pay for all of us. They picked my oldest brother and younger sister. I was disappointed because I loved school, but I understood that their hands were tied. I'm sure they wanted all of us to get the education we needed, but it just wasn't possible.

One night when we were sleeping we heard a loud knock on our door. Men were shouting and telling us to open the door. My first instinct was to jump out of bed and get my sisters and slide under the bed. Who could this be? Did the killers track us down? This is the end. We wouldn't be able to survive. My mother woke up and went to open the door. Four men from the country police walked in with knives and pistols. Who do we call for help when we need help? Congo's 911. This is how the conversation would go:

Operator: Hello, this is 911. Please state your emergency.

Caller: Yes, please help. We are being robbed.

Operator: Yes, I know. I'm robbing you, dummy!

Caller: Awkward . . .

Talk about insanity. They demanded money, but my mother told them she had no money. They didn't believe her, and one of them held a knife to her neck and told her to give him money or she would be killed. I saw them slapping my mother repeatedly and demanding money. Finally, my mother went in her bedroom and gave them $100 that my father had left her. This money was to support us until my father's return, if he ever returned alive. He was in Kenya trying to find refuge for us. This money wasn't enough for them. They came into our room and looked around. I told my sisters to be quiet as I saw the men's heavy boots make their way across our room. Our room was empty except for the bed and a few pieces of clothing on the floor. It never occurred to them to check under the bed. They left and went back to the living room.

Throughout this whole ordeal, my brother was sleeping on a mattress in a corner in the living room. One of the policemen must have thought there was money under the mattress because he picked it up and threw it across the room. My poor brother flew across the room with the mattress and landed on it perfectly and just kept sleeping as if nothing had happened. I have to admit that I chuckled a little. How could he not wake up? Was he still alive? Due to malnutrition, cholera, typhoid, and other diseases, people, especially children, would go to sleep and never wake up. I started thinking that maybe he was dead, but he was very much alive the next morning and didn't know what had happened. Thank God! I want to be in such a deep sleep myself the next time something like this occurs!

Living in Congo was eventful. One day one of the Rwandan families that lived across from us made some mandazi (fried dough) and decided to sell it downtown to make a little money. The father of the family wore a simple button-down shirt, some shorts, and worn-out leather shoes. When he returned, we realized that he had no shirt and no shoes. He walked in the house half-naked. We asked him what had happened, and he said the police had attacked him, took his mandazi, his shirt, and stole his shoes right off his feet! I laughed, and you can laugh, too, because it's funny!

One day my mother washed our clothes that included one of my semi-nice dresses. She put the clothes on the line to dry, but they were gone when she came to get them in the evening. She wasn't happy and told us what had happened. We automatically knew who had stolen the dress. A

Congolese boy in the neighborhood was known to steal people's things. He was about eight years old and would enter people's homes and steal cooked food, matches, clothing, and women's underwear—anything he could find. His mother was so sick of this behavior that she lit a fire and put his little hands in the fire to prevent him from stealing, but that didn't stop him. We told my mother that the boy had taken the dress, and she was determined to get it back!

The next morning we were all sitting outside and saw someone wearing my dress coming toward us! My mother got up and put her hands on her hips and waited patiently for her prey. As this person got closer, we realized it was the little boy. He was walking so proudly as if he were on Project Runway. As soon as he reached us, my mother took him by the dress, undressed him, and took it. The boy ran back to his house totally naked. We all laughed so hard. The next day he was caught stealing again. Poor child!

One morning I went to Lake Kivu to wash some clothes and fetch water to take home. We used the water to cook, wash clothes, and clean the dishes. This water was not very clean, but we had no choice. Because of the large number of dead bodies on the streets, people decided to throw them into the water to clear the roads. It was very hard to differentiate a log from a dead body in the water. As I was washing my clothes in the lake, the current took away one of my favorite shirts. I didn't much to wear, so I wasn't going to let this shirt go. I couldn't swim, but I saw a log in the water, got on top of it, and moved my arms to get closer to the shirt. When I almost reached it, I stretched and made a little jump to catch the shirt. The jump made the log turn over, and I realized that I had been on top of a corpse the entire time! I quickly turned around and actually swam to shore. I didn't know I could swim. You learn something new every day! I swam once in my life on that day, and then I forgot how to swim!

After I collected myself, I filled a jerry can with water, placed it on my head, and put my clothing on top. I put on my flip-flops and started heading home. The walk home was about an hour, and I had to cross a busy road. It was customary for kids my age to walk for hours to go grocery shopping, fetch water, and do other chores. At the age of eight, I was pretty much doing many things that adults do. Still traumatized from what had just happened at the lake, I couldn't wait to get home. I was walking so fast that I crossed the busy street without noticing a motorcycle approaching me. Realizing he was about to hit me, the motorcyclist got angry. He jumped off and ran after me.

All I could think of was that this man was going to catch me, rape me, and then kill me. I couldn't let that happen. I quickly dropped the clothing and jerry can on the ground, took off my flip-flops, and ran for my life. I was running as fast as my little feet could take me, but he was faster. I couldn't outrun him, and suddenly I felt his footsteps right behind me. He grabbed me with one hand and beat me so hard that I started wondering if he was insane. He tore my shirt and continued to punch me in the face and ribs. I screamed and screamed, and when he was finally satisfied, he dropped me to the ground and went back to his motorcycle. I stood up, tried to take the dirt off my clothes and face, walked back to get my flip-flops and jerry can, and quietly made my way back home. When I arrived, my mother asked what had happened. I told her that I had fallen. The look she gave me said that she didn't believe me, but she didn't ask any more questions. I'm sure she was praising God that I was still alive because that's exactly what I was also doing—thanking God for my life!

A few days after the beating my father came and moved us into a refugee camp in Congo. This wasn't a "summer camp" or a fun adventure. Go to the University of Google (UOG) at www.google.com and type "Congo refugee camps" in the search engine, and click on the "images" button. This will give you an idea of what a refugee camp looks like. This place is where I saw so many children die that I really thought my time had come. Why wouldn't I die like the rest? I was not any more special. We moved from camp to camp looking for a "safer" place to stay—a place with less malaria, less death, and fewer killings. Hundreds of us would go to sleep, but only a handful would wake up. I later became scared of going to sleep because I was afraid I would die. The more dead bodies, the more toxic the environment became, so we would get up, leave the dead bodies, and move to a different camp. Some people would walk around the dead bodies and take clothes off the bodies so that they could at least have a change of clothes. Some even went into the clothing business. People were hustling to make money any way they could.

Every morning we would wake up with an empty cup and stand in line that seemed to go on forever to get our morsel of porridge. I would try to look over the shoulders of the other kids and adults to see if any of it would be left by the time I got in front. This particular event has stayed in my mind to the point that I hate waiting in line for food. At weddings or any other events that require people to stand in line to get food, I either have someone make a plate for me, or I wait until there is no line and serve myself. We needed to find a way to leave this place or we would not survive. God heard our prayers and made a way for us to go to Kenya.

Breaking in Kenya

Living in Kenya wasn't so bad. When we first arrived, we lived in a decent house in a decent town for about four months. As my family ran out of money, we would move into a less expensive house. Money would be tight again, and we would look for an even cheaper house. My mother gave birth to the youngest of my siblings in Kenya, which meant that our family of two adults and eight children was moving at least once a year to find more affordable housing. It came to a point that my younger brother, the one who slept through a home invasion, would wake up every morning and be gone for hours only to come back and tell us he was looking for an even cheaper house for us. Mind you, he was 10 years old! By the time we left Kenya, we were living in a 3-room house. The living room, which served as a dining room and children's bedroom, the kitchen, and my parents' room. Because of the lack of sleeping space, I slept on a blanket on the floor every night for the five years we were in Kenya. We used a common bathroom with other residents that lived in the building. Ten people were living in a 3-room house. Somehow, we made it work!

My siblings and I were very fortunate to all be able to attend school in Kenya. People who we will never meet, people of God who decided to make a change in the lives of refugees, paid for our schooling. I was thrilled because I loved school. I was a gifted student, which allowed my parents to move me from second grade to fourth grade and then from sixth grade to high school!

My three siblings and I went to the same primary school, Imara Primary School, a few miles down the road from our house. Kenyan students would get money from their parents to buy lunch, which usually consisted of French fries and a really delicious tomato sauce. My parents could not afford to give each of us money, so my mother would put leftovers from dinner, usually rice and beans, into a big bowl, and my siblings and I would all meet during lunchtime in my older brother's classroom and eat from the bowl together! Students would come from their classes and stand around us and laugh! They would mock us, saying we were poor and eating from a cooking pan! This happened every single school day, but we got used to it, and it became part of life. We had no choice. My parents could only afford to buy us bread on Sunday. They really tried to do this every Sunday unless money was extremely tight, and then we would only drink porridge on Sundays.

Going to this school wasn't all that bad for me. Since I was a gifted and well-behaved student, my teachers picked me to be the class prefect, asked me to write notes on the blackboard for all students because I had the best handwriting in the class, and I received many achievement awards!

One of my proudest moments in this school occurred when I was the third student in class one year despite missing a whole semester. One morning my older brother decided not to make porridge for everyone before he went to school. Being the good caring sister, I decided to make the porridge even though it wasn't my turn. I was already dressed to go to school and had on white socks and black dress shoes. As I was cooking the porridge, I tripped on a bowl of hot boiling water, and the water spilled in my shoes through my socks. I screamed, and my parents came running from their bedroom to the kitchen and found me on the floor. My father carried me to the simple mattress that was on the floor in the living room, and my mother took off my shoes and socks. As she was pulling off the socks, the skin on my left ankle came off with the sock! My father put me on his back and walked thirty minutes to the hospital. I stayed home for a whole semester because my wound wouldn't heal.

Halfway into the school semester, my father decided I had missed too much school and told me to try to leave. He found two long wooden sticks and showed me how to hop on them. This is how I was going to get to school. I would hop my way there for almost an hour. When my father asked you to do something, you did it. No ifs, ands, or buts. I took my wooden sticks and hopped for about ten minutes, but I finally got tired and decided to sit on a large rock and rest. While I was resting, two of the teachers passed by and felt sorry for me, so they decided to carry me the rest of the way to school. I sat on the floor the whole day because sitting on a chair was impossible. I needed to lay my leg flat. My teachers carried me home from school and told my parents that I should stay home.

The following week my father asked me to send a letter to my teacher asking her to send me notes of all the lessons that were being taught to my classmates so that I wouldn't fall behind. Every week a student would bring notes, and I would sit at home, do the work, and teach myself. A week before the semester was over I felt well enough to go to school and take the exam. When the results came out, I was amazed to hear my name called as the third student in class! My whole family was so proud of me!

Dancing for Food and Healing

My sister and I joined a refugee dance group in Nairobi, Kenya. This was a very talented group of Rwandan refugees that got so big that we were traveling all over the country to dance for presidents and other important figures. Missionaries from the Western world would come to see us dance. Many of them were touched to see so many refugee children dancing with big smiles on their faces despite everything they had gone through. The dance teacher would pinch us under our armpits if we didn't position our hands the right way or if we didn't smile while dancing. Anything short of perfection would earn us a pinch.

I would go to dance practice every day and endure the pain for two reasons: I knew that at the end of the month the group would provide us with bags of rice and beans to take home and share with our families. I was happy to see that I was somehow contributing to the family. I could see my parents struggling every day to keep a smile on our faces, and I was happy to help. The second reason was to escape from reality and all the other painful events that were taking place in my life. Dancing was my high! I felt that I was untouchable, and that the world was full of nothing but happiness. I still have a passion for dancing traditional Rwandan music and all other types of music. I've held workshops around the country on traditional Rwandan dancing. You can see a clip of our dance group on YouTube at https://www.youtube.com/watch?v=n7owH1SISKQ.

You probably can't recognize me, but I'm shown at 0:28 seconds and 2:48 seconds. Back then I was like a skinny model, according to Western standards, only because I was malnourished. Now I'm the exact opposite! I'm the tall girl second from the left in the back row! I have moves like Mick Jagger!

Murder of My Aunt's Family

Two years before we were granted visas to come to the USA as refugees my family received horrible news. I had been used to people dying around me due to AIDS, robberies, police attacks in refugee settlements, and other horrible reasons. These experiences were part of life. Once you have gone through tragic events so many times, it becomes your new normal. Tragedy was my normal, but this news really hit me.

In 1997, my aunt, my mother's younger sister, had a baby. A couple of days after she had been discharged from the hospital she was sleeping in her bedroom with the baby, while her husband, all her children except for one, and my uncle, who had gone to visit them to share the good news that he had received a scholarship to go to France, were sitting in the living room. They heard a loud knock on the door, and as soon as my aunt's husband opened the door, he was shot in the head. My uncle quickly grabbed my cousin, shoved him into a corner, and stood right in front of him. The men fired a couple bullets at both of them. The bullets went through my uncle and my cousin, and they both fell down. The men didn't bother to look in the other rooms. They left the bodies on the floor, switched off the light, and left.

My aunt had been listening to everything in horror in her bedroom. After waiting a few minutes to make sure the men were gone, she woke up, went into the living room, and switched on the light. She started screaming in agony at the scene before her. The men happened to look back and saw the light in the house. They were sure they had switched it off and decided to go back to double-check. They found my aunt holding her one-week-old baby in the living room and crying hysterically. They snatched the baby away from my aunt, stepped on the baby, and her tender little body exploded. Then they raped my aunt and killed her.

They made sure no one else was in the house and turned off the light and left.

In the early morning, neighbors came to the house to see what had happened. Again, this was normal event, as things like this happened so often that it became a ritual. The neighbors looked through the house, and as they were about to leave, my cousin who had been shielded by my uncle in the corner spoke. He told the neighbors that by the grace of God he was still alive. He had played dead and heard everything that was being done to his mother. No one knew the killers, no one was allowed to talk about this subject, and no one was allowed to investigate. This was politically motivated, and these neighbors weren't politicians. All they knew is that their dear friends had been killed, and they didn't do it! To this day, he is handicapped and still has one bullet in his shoulder. The neighbors took him and cared for him. He later went to live with my grandmother and his younger brother who had been visiting her during the tragedy. My grandmother became their new mother until she passed away in 2014. These young men have gone through so much, and my wish is that they can come to the United States one day. With faith, I know that God will make it happen.

The Letter

After five years of applying for resettlement in the USA and being rejected, we finally received a letter saying we had been approved to come in 1999. Going to America was very important for us. I cannot stress this enough. For those of you who have been born and raised in America, you are in a country where many refugees want to be. Families who received this letter and flooded the streets rejoicing would be in jail the following morning or even dead. What happened in this case is that this letter caused our neighbors to be jealous. They had waited for their letters for years. As soon as they found out you received the letter, someone would talk to someone who would talk to someone else, and suddenly the police are at your door taking you to jail for a crime you had supposedly committed. I remember one man was almost beaten to death and wasn't able to come to America because of his injury.

Receiving this letter was important because of all the money and energy that my family had spent trying to get settled in the USA. For a family to be given refugee status to come to the USA, each family had to go through an extensive interview process. Each family member would be interviewed alone to see if his/her story would be consistent with the story of the other family members to make sure no one was lying just to get a free ticket to the USA. Each time my family applied we would be interviewed at least four times. We would then be denied settlement, and we would apply again the following year. In our case, we applied five times, which meant an average of forty expensive trips of ten people in a bus. Before we left home for the interview, we would spend at least one hour praying and singing one particular praise song in French. Every time we would be denied resettlement my younger brother would say that the song was bad luck, and we needed to find another song!

My parents sat us down and firmly told us that we were not to tell anyone about the letter. This was very hard because we were very excited. I wanted to go outside and scream and dance and run and throw myself at something because I was so happy and invincible. I would be in America soon!

I remember one of my brothers sitting on a stool in our living room/dining room/bedroom saying how he would be sitting on a couch watching television with a remote in his hand! That's what excited him the most—sitting on a couch. He basically wanted to be a couch potato! He is far from being a couch potato now. He is a computer engineer!

What excited me the most about coming to America was that I would have white friends. I would be able to play with their soft hair. I would talk like them, and I would even marry a white boy one day! Being white in Africa was important. White people were thought to be prettier, closer to God, rich, and didn't need to shower because they were always clean. Having a white friend was gold. My younger sister and I would play a game of "eating like white people." We would sit elegantly and take forks and eat as if we were royalty and try not to spill anything on our clothes because white people weren't messy! In Africa, everyone wanted to be your friend if you had white friends. I went to school with a couple of them and befriended them, so I was considered to be the "bomb." Going to a country with white people all around me was just insane. Be ready for me, America. Here comes Clementine!

Breaking in the United States

As the plane landed on U.S. soil, I couldn't wait to get out. I wanted to jump out of the plane before it stopped. I looked outside the tiny window and saw white people everywhere! I was tired from hours and hours of flying over an ocean that seemed to go on forever. We were fed chicken that tasted like rubber, and all I was thinking was that white people eat rubber chicken to keep them white and allow them to grow long hair. I'm sure there was chicken for black people, one that tasted like what we ate back in Africa. Little did I know that the chicken had been injected with different chemicals, which accounted for the taste. Oh my! Needless to say, I never found black people chicken! I found all types of chicken, all natural, organic, regular chicken, overweight chicken, (turkey) etc. The choices in America are endless.

I was surprised to see that I was already a celebrity when I arrived in America. American people were very hospitable. Every time they would ask me my name, they would start singing "Oh My Darling, Clementine." These Americans had practiced a song just for me! America was treating me like royalty. One day I went to the grocery store and found oranges with my name on them too. WOW! I was important! There is a song and now oranges. What else? Is there a car? Is the car orange? Can I have it?

Culture Shock

The first encounter I had with a white person was pleasant. As I was lying in bed one day, my sister came running into my room and told me that I had a white visitor. I was so excited. I asked my sister how old the visitor looked, and she told me she looked my age. YES! My first white friend! I quickly glanced at myself in the mirror to see if I looked presentable and headed downstairs. As soon as I opened the front door, I found this beautiful white lady with long hair that seemed to go on forever and blue or green eyes. She was sitting on the floor with a dog. Her name was Lee Snead. What a beautiful woman! I introduced myself, and she gave me a huge hug, and she smelled really great! I just stared at her hair. I stared and stared and stared. I just had to touch that hair. Would she let me? She had to. She was my first white friend. My brain would tell me to just put my hand out and touch it, but my body wouldn't move, so I kept staring. I'm in America!

It turned out that Lee was not my age but rather my mother's age! Although she had a daughter my age, Tina, Lee and I became close friends. She introduced us to her family, took us to stores to buy toiletries, took us to church to meet other wonderful white folks, and brought us clothes, shoes, and food. Most importantly, I finally got to touch her beautiful hair as much as I wanted. In fact, my whole family, from my father down to my youngest sibling, would hover around her and stroke her hair. We were petting her like the family pet. Lee was the best thing that happened to us when we got to America. I love Lee, I love her family, and I see Jesus in her every time we meet.

Education

Getting assimilated into American culture wasn't easy. I had such a difficult time that sometimes I wished I could go home. This feeling was not something I shared with many people. I have always tried to be strong on the outside and remain positive, even though I would be hurting on the inside, but it was hard. When I first got to the U.S., I was enrolled in the eighth grade at a local Catholic school in Dayton, Ohio. I was at the school for only a couple of semesters before I went to high school. This was my first interaction with American children and teachers. The first thing that surprised me and made me very uncomfortable was the amount of disrespect the kids had toward their teachers.

In my culture, your teacher is like a parent. Your teacher also knew your parent. If you misbehaved, your teacher would spank you, call your parents before you got home from school, and as soon as you arrived home, your parents would spank you as well. It takes a village to raise a child, and our culture takes this very seriously. I thought that being a teacher in America must be the hardest thing to do. Students would sit in class and pass gas loudly. They would make faces while the teacher was writing on the board. They would cuss in class, and they would yell at the teachers. It was awful. I felt so ashamed and embarrassed even though I wasn't the one doing any of these things. One of my proudest moments in elementary school was being selected to compete in the National Spelling Bee just a couple of weeks after I arrived. The students must have been surprised to see a refugee kid who barely spoke English being selected to be part of the spelling bee. My parents were so proud!

High School

High school was a NIGHTMARE! I couldn't wait to graduate. These were the most miserable four years of my life. I went to a very good private Catholic high school in Dayton and received a superb education, but some of the students were awful. We were teenagers. In general, teenagers can be mean, especially when they don't understand you because you are somehow different. When I was in school, I was a different person from when I was at home. In high school, I was very shy, antisocial, and depressed. I just hated it. There were all these cliques that I couldn't seem to join. Students barely spoke to me because I was different. Some were outright mean to me for no reason. I remember one particular student who was so awful to me that it was almost as if I had killed her pet or something. Even now whenever I see her on Facebook I want to ask what her problem was, but I stop and say a quick prayer.

When I went to school, I wore second-hand shoes and clothing. I was relieved that we had to wear a uniform, but we were also allowed to wear whatever we wanted on Friday. I would fake being sick so that I didn't have to go to school. The kids would make fun of me. Lunchtime was the worst. I felt that I had nowhere to sit. No one invited me to their table, but I quickly realized that all the African-American students would sit on one side, and all the whites would sit on the other side. This happened automatically, and I don't even think the students knew they were doing it. I decided to sit at one of the tables on the African-American side because they looked more like me. I don't think the black and the white students disliked each other because they would talk in the hallways and in class, but this segregation just seemed to happen. Sometimes during lunch I would go into the bathroom and lock myself in a stall and just wait until lunch period was over before going back to class. I didn't want to deal with the confusion in the cafeteria. The interesting thing is that the white students were generally nicer and more welcoming to me than the black students. I thought it would be the other way around. Needless to say, the very few friends I had in high school were white.

High school students were worse than elementary school students in terms of respecting authority. Again, I felt embarrassed by some of the things the students did, and I decided to not be part of it at all. I closed in and never opened up. I had my own pain that none of these students would understand. They worried about having cell phones and the latest shoes, while I worried about receiving a phone call from Rwanda and being told that one of our relatives had been killed or was "missing." They were worried about boyfriends and girlfriends and going to the prom, while I worried about not being made fun of and hoping the day would end quickly so that I could go home and be myself.

I never attended any school dances, including the prom. I was never invited to any of the parties the students had, and I was called all sorts of names, including weirdo, freak, and ugly. Ugly? Yes, ugly. I had never considered myself to be an ugly person, but someone had just called me ugly. The real Clementine would say something. She would not let someone talk to her in that manner, and she would make sure this person learned his or her lesson, even if a fight happened. The high school Clementine, however, said nothing. She felt sad and defeated. All she could wait for was graduation day when all the misery would end. I remember one day around prom time that I asked one of the students if she was going to prom. Everyone was doing it. Everyone was asking everyone. Most people were asking others to go to the prom with them as their dates, but I was merely just asking this student to strike up a conversation. I will never forget what she told me. She said, "I'm not going to the prom. No one has asked me. Look how ugly I am. Who would want to ask me out? "Whoa! Two "ugly" people conversing! She's a keeper. Misery likes company! She should be my

BFF! I wonder who else wanted to be on "team ugly." I had some serious recruiting to do!

The difference between us was that she truly believed she was ugly. How did she come to that conclusion? I don't know, but I'm pretty sure the students at school were partly to blame. On the other hand, I didn't believe I was ugly. These students just didn't know me. I couldn't let them get to me. No way, Jose! I don't really blame the students because I was not the "cool" type in high school, and neither did I want to be. I was this shy, quiet student who did well in class but had a freaky accent. I don't think I would have wanted to be my friend either. Out of everything I had gone through the previous years, my high school years were the hardest four years of my life and continue to be. The bullying was real. What kept me strong was knowing that I was worthy and the loving community that waited for me as soon as I stepped out of school. The one thing that was missing during these years in high school was LOVE. There was no love.

If you are reading this and have been bullied or are being bullied, I want you to understand that this is not the end of the world. This is a phase, and you will make it out just fine. People's opinions of you are not your business, and as long as you know your true worth and that you are a unique masterpiece, no one can take that from you. Because of your resilience, you will most likely turn out to be an amazing person, and all those who are bullying you now will have regrets— regrets you will not have! Take this as an opportunity to show the world what you are made of and grow and flourish!

If you are reading this book and you are bullying someone, stop it because it's useless and pointless. You found yourself in this world just like the person you are bullying did. You did not ask to be born. You will leave this world the way you came in just like the one you are bullying. You don't have the formula of life, and neither does the person you are bullying. Your life can change in a heartbeat, and you could be in the other person's shoes. What would you want written on your tombstone? S/he was the best bully ever? Did you know that the most powerful and successful people think as far ahead as what will be written on their tombstone and try to live a life that reflects the message they want?

When I was in Rwanda before the war, I lived a very luxurious life. My family had maids that did everything for us. My parents could afford anything I wanted, and I could have been a bully, but I wasn't because I would have to report to my parents who were very devoted Christians, and I was terrified of doing the wrong thing. On the other hand, I had friends who were equally as rich and popular but who bullied other less fortunate students. During the war, we all lost everything and lived in a refugee camp similar to the one photographed on the cover of this book. Next to me on the ground lying naked and crying is the student who was bullying the other students! Bullying does not make anyone cool. It makes others disgusted by you. I challenge you to wake up one day and decide to stop the bullying. Start being nice to those you bully and see how much cooler and popular you will be! You will feel good about yourself, and everyone will be looking at you as an exemplary person. You will never regret this decision.

College

Attending college was one of the happiest moments in my life. The real Clementine started to come out and shine. I met students from all over the world. I was understood more. I was appreciated, loved, and I blossomed. Students I had gone to high school with started seeing a different side of Clementine. Some of them even approached me and said they didn't want to be friends with me in high school because I didn't talk to anyone, and that I looked mean. Who knew I was seen as the mean one in high school?

The University of Dayton opened so many doors for me, and I started living again. I would share my story with students and professors, and they would listen. I started going on stage and did public speaking. I LOVED it. I made people laugh, I loved people, I inspired people and, most importantly, I started healing. Speaking was therapy to me. Every time after giving a speech I felt free. I wanted to scream out in joy. I got involved in many organizations and formed my own organization, the Afrika Club. I recruited diverse students to be part of this club. We held conferences and invited the community to come and hear from survivors of wars, to watch us dance, and to fight for human rights together. This was my dream come true. Some of the high school students joined the club. I appeared in university publications that promoted diversity, which were distributed all over the world. The university president and his staff knew me. I was finally part of a community!

Below is one of the many publications about me. My last name is different because my "ugly" self found someone to marry, and I changed my last name to his, which is much shorter to write and pronounce anyway!

The Marianist language crosses all dialects.

CLÉMENTINE IGILIBAMBE

fled war-ravaged Rwanda when she was eight years old. She lived in refugee camps in Zaire and then

Kenya. She speaks five languages. Yet enrolling at a U.S. college still intimidated her.

Thankfully, she was enrolling at the University of Dayton, where a robust Center for International Programs helped to ease her fears. "Everyone here is so welcoming. Tutors helped with language and classes. The International Student Club helped me adjust but also let me teach U.S. students about being a student abroad."

While pursuing a human rights and international studies degree, Igilibambe brought a piece of her upbringing to southwest Ohio when she founded a UD Afrika Club. The club allowed her to share her heritage — from native cuisine to beloved African dance — with students on campus. And with Igilibambe's involvement in Student Leadership Council, World Youth Alliance and U.N. Agents of Change, she represents the student of tomorrow: ambitious, worldly and committed to transforming the world.

Fat, Fat, Fat

Why do so many people here in America call each other "fat"? I quickly realized that when people got mad at each other, they called each other fat. In my culture, being fat was a good thing. A fat woman was regarded as healthy, more likely to bear children, and come from a rich family. I found that here in America attitudes are the opposite. One thing that frustrates my father is when he sees any of the women in my family losing weight. He would ask if we had enough food and talk about it a lot. When my father sees me and compliments me on how "good" I look, I know it's time to go on a diet. When he tells me I look bad, then I know I'm on the right track.

Being fat almost cost my brother his life one day! One of his "girlfriends" from Rwanda arrived in the USA a couple of years before we arrived. As soon as he arrived in the U.S., he decided he was going to sweet-talk his "girlfriend" and tell her how beautiful she was. He proceeded to tell her that she was so fat and beautiful like a fattened cow, and that she had big hips. You can imagine how the rest of the story went. They never dated!

Elders are Golden. Treat Them Like Gold.

One thing I quickly realized is that elders are treated differently in the USA. Their lives are somehow different from those of the general population. Most of them don't live in their own homes anymore. They live in nursing homes. I was honored and privileged to meet some elders in the community when I was working for a health insurance company. I met elders who lived in nursing homes with no one coming to visit them for years, even though they had many children. I met with elders who were living in public housing because their children tricked them into selling their home to them for one dollar and were promised to live in the basement but were later kicked out. I met elders who were forced to go into a nursing home because their children felt they were a burden to them. I met elders who were veterans and homeless and had no one to care for them. They were sleeping on the street and begging for food during the day.

I had never encountered a homeless person in Africa. Our community simply does not let anyone be homeless when they can just sleep on the floor in your home. The community comes together to figure out a solution. It was rare for someone to commit suicide in my culture. The sense of community and supporting one another helped people remain mentally stable.

In my culture, elders are "golden." There is a reason why they are in their "golden years." They have life experience and knowledge that one will never receive in school. In my country, our parents take care of us in their homes, and we take care of them in our homes when it's our turn. Elders are wise, and they help shape us to be better people, better leaders, and better parents either by learning from their mistakes or from their accomplishments. This way, if a community has been intact, we don't need to reinvent the wheel. We respect and love them dearly for that. The older they get, the better, just like a fine wine. It's funny how we keep old wine and cherish it but don't think of human beings that way. If I needed advice from a life expert, I would go to an elder on their deathbed. I am confident they would have the best advice for me, and that it would have something to do with love and community.

Community

If you are reading this and feel you don't have a community that cares for you, one that you can connect with and one that truly supports you, stop reading and find one. You need to belong, my friend. Community is everything. The Internet has made things easy for us. Countless websites, such as Facebook and Meetup, have made it possible for people to belong in groups they can identify with. My favorite is Meetup.com because once you are part of a group you actually engage in activities with the people in your group. You actually meet. If you cannot identify with any groups, create one of your own. Some of you might be thinking that this is the most miserable thing you have ever heard of because you are not outgoing; you are shy, and you are an introvert. Stop those thoughts! You can be all those things and still belong in a community. Create a community for shy and introverted people in which you can meet and sit and stare at each other in silence. I don't care. You need to belong.

Human beings are social beings, so go ahead and socialize. You will feel much better. I promise!

Age

Why is it that people in the USA are afraid to discuss their age? I quickly learned that asking a person their age, especially a woman who seems to be older than you are, is a no-no. Yet, we see people doing all sorts of things to stay alive longer. If there were an injection that people could receive to add ten years to their lives, the country would quickly run out of the supply. People don't want to get older. Make up your mind. Do you want to live longer, or do you want to die? The math is simple. The longer you live, the older you get. Every year you live you get a year older. So, don't get offended when people ask your age. Say it with pride because you have life lessons to share. God has blessed you with your years so that you can finish your mission in this world. Hiding or denying your age is not part of your mission. If God told you He wanted to take you home now, you would probably beg to stay alive. You are wise, and you can do so much good by mentoring those younger than you are, especially high school students who bully. Yes, I know I'm biased!

Ridiculous Happiness

During the summer of 2014, I really started thinking about my life, my purpose, my passion, and my calling. I recalled what I had gone through in my life and thought . . . wow, what a journey I'm on . . . What a Life!

What happened that summer that made me rethink my life? The summer ended well, and it led to ridiculous happiness!

On July 23, 2014, I went to the Labor and Delivery Room at UMass Memorial Hospital in Worcester, Massachusetts, and was informed that my baby girl, who my family and I were looking forward to spending Thanksgiving with, had died in my womb. She was 28 weeks. She just stopped breathing just like that! Her name was Clarette Belle. As we were finishing with the funeral and grieving, my father-in-law passed away. Two weeks later my grandmother passed away. We were grieving the loss of three deaths all at once, but I was still focused on my daughter's death. Going through labor and the usual changes that take place in a woman's body after childbirth, such as milk production, were affecting me, even though I had no child. Obviously, my body did not get the memo that my lovely daughter was gone. This was the hardest part of grieving.

Clarette had been part of our lives already. Every night before going to sleep we would sit and pray for each other, including Clarette. My three-year-old son would always rub my belly and talk to his unborn sister. Every day after I returned home from work he would run to me and give me my hug and give Clarette her hug. He loved to feel her move inside my belly. He was so excited about being a big brother that every time he did something commendable we would tell him that he was a good boy, but he would say, "No, mommy, I'm a good brother."

My whole stay at the UMass Medical Center felt unreal. I was in so much shock that people would come to see me and be shocked at what they saw. Normally, when you see someone who has just lost a loved one, you expect tears and sadness. Sometimes, it can even be uncomfortable because one never knows the right words to say. In my case, I was in so much shock that I was cracking jokes the whole time I had visitors. I was such a happy and strong person, or so people thought, that it was very easy for them to deal with me. Visitors came in my room sad but left happy. The medical staff at the hospital treated me as though I was the only patient, and we quickly became a small family. I almost didn't want to go home because I didn't want to face reality. I loved being in the hospital.

One night as I was lying in my hospital bed I felt restless and tired of being in bed all the time, so I decided to take a walk on my floor. When I got outside my room, I realized that a purple card was on my door. I walked over to the nurses' station and asked one of the nurses about the card. She told me it meant I had lost a baby. I decided to walk around the whole floor to count how many of us had lost babies. I made one round and came to a door with the purple card. I stood outside and felt so sad for the family. Why did this have to happen to another family? I stood there and said a quick prayer of strength for the family and was about ready to head back to my room when the nurse came and asked if I was okay. I told her I was fine and that I was just saying a quick prayer for this other family that had lost a child. She looked at me concerned and asked, "What do you mean? We only have one loss on the floor, darling. This is your room!" Oh my! I looked at the room number, and it was really my room. "I see," I quickly said and went back inside. Of all the women who had delivered children that day, I was the only one who had lost a baby. I was the chosen one. For what? Why was I the one? Was God teaching me some kind of lesson? I did not comprehend many things, and I had so many questions, but I had to trust that everything happens for a reason. God gives and God takes.

After I was discharged from the hospital, I went home, and my son ran to me. He had missed his mom. I was in the hospital for about three days, so my family and friends kept him home. He was so excited to see me and followed me to my bedroom. I was exhausted and wanted to be alone. With all the people who were coming in and out, it was hard for me to be alone, but I appreciated them being there. I sat down on my bed, and my son came to me and gave me a big hug. He then proceeded to touch my belly to give baby Clarette a hug. I couldn't help it. I tried to be so strong for my son, but I couldn't. I started to cry, and he looked at me in shock. He asked, "Mommy, what's wrong? What's wrong? I'm gonna help you. Don't worry, Christon is here." This made me cry even harder. What a sweet boy God had blessed me with. I told him that Clarette was in heaven, and she was no longer in my belly. He didn't seem to understand what I was saying, so I just told him that Clarette was gone, and we would visit her one day. A couple of weeks later I explained to him what heaven was and told him that God and Jesus and angels and his grandpa and his great grandma were all in heaven. I told him that heaven is a happy place, and we will see them one day. He seemed to understand a little better. Even now Christon does not allow us to tell him he is a "good boy." He still insists that he is a "good brother."

Losing a child HURTS. You never think of burying your own child, and when it happens, and it happens every day, your whole life shatters, and you have many unanswered questions. When I lost my little girl, I was angry, confused, depressed, and zombie-like all at the same time. I could go through several emotional states in just a minute. My emotions were unpredictable, and I was scared.

A couple of weeks after I buried my daughter I was wondering when the pain would go away. I talked to a lot of people who had gone through the same thing, and they told me that it gets better, but the pain never really goes away. I was angry with myself for not healing fast enough. I wanted time to go by fast so that I could heal and have a normal life. I'm actually not a very patient person. I'm also my worst critic, and I expected to get better ASAP. Little did I know that I have no control over such things. Family and friends would come over to offer comfort, and I would try to be strong and smile, but as soon as they left, I would sit in my little corner and cry helplessly. No one or nothing could take away this pain.

I thought that going to church would solve my problems, but I didn't think that such a church existed. I grew up a Catholic and had been to so many masses that I felt could say mass on my own, but female priests aren't allowed in the Catholic Church. I felt that I needed a different kind of experience—a church that would speak to me. I wanted to feel as if the pastor/priest knew all my troubles and was talking directly to me. I didn't want to explain myself. I wanted to be welcomed and held and told that everything would be okay and that someone understands. I decided to try other denominations before I went back to the Catholic Church.

I felt that I was betraying my church and family for investigating other religions, but it was either this or I was going to lose it. I asked a couple of friends where they attended church and also did my own research online. I decided to go to one church a friend suggested and another I found out about online. I made sure the services were at different times on Sunday so that I could attend both in one day. The first church was mostly attended by fellow Africans and was led by a very energetic female pastor. When I walked in, the congregation was praising. The music was extremely loud, and everyone seemed to be speaking very loudly in foreign tongues. The church itself was very small. Coming from a Catholic background where things are subtle and mellow, this was a totally new experience for me. I left five minutes after arriving because I was beginning to have a headache.

The second church was the opposite. Anyone could get up and go up front and preach. It seemed as though the church was looking for people to volunteer to preach. People would raise their hands and get on stage and preach. I felt very uncomfortable, but I tried very hard to "feel the spirit" and stay. Maybe the good part was coming. I waited five more minutes, but the good part never came. Patience is not my biggest virtue, so I got up and left. I went outside and sat in my car and cried in frustration. Why could I not find a church that fits me? Am I that complicated? I drove home very disappointed and decided to go to a Catholic church the following Sunday. I decided to stay with what I already knew.

I hate giving up. I knew that somewhere a church was waiting for me. I decided to try again. I asked coworkers for advice. I asked them to help me or I would go nuts. I needed an intervention. I started feeling as though I was going to end my life, so I would get in the car and drive just to drive. I would drive not knowing exactly where I was going. One day I sat in the car and decided I was going to drive the twelve hours to Ohio to visit my family. I then changed my mind and parked in a parking lot facing a big wall and wondered how it would feel if I just turned on the engine and pushed the gas as hard as I could and slammed into the wall. I wouldn't feel any pain. I would be free. Then it hit me. I have a wonderful husband and a three-year-old. What about them? What about the pain they would have? My husband needed me more than ever before, as he was also mourning the loss of his daughter. This was not about me. I drove home and hugged my husband and son and went to sleep. I would resume the church hunt the following day.

The next day a coworker told me that she knew of a church that she thought I would like. I asked her if she had ever attended the church, and she said she hadn't. Oh boy! OK. What was I to lose? I decided to attend the church the following

Sunday. Lifesong Church was about twenty minutes from my house in a town called Sutton. This church changed my life! When I walked into the church lobby, I felt that I finally belonged. A sense of peace washed over me. When I entered the main church, I found an energetic band praising and the congregation singing in unison. All of a sudden, I felt so happy. I sang and praised and smiled and cried at the same time. I didn't want this experience to end. I felt that this is what heaven would feel like.

The church was running a series called "7 Stories," which featured life stories of different church members who had led hard difficult lives but were able to overcome their problems. I felt that I was listening to my own life story. I felt connected. The pastor was even better. He spoke the truth. He spoke to me. I didn't want the service to end. I wanted to stay right there. At one point, I even thought that if God decided to take me right there, I would go straight to heaven. Sunday had become and still is the best day of my week. I decided I had to be alive throughout the week so that I could attend church on Sunday. No more driving into the wall nonsense. I counted the days and even hours until the next service. I was alive! Watch out world, Clementine was back!

At church, I learned that I needed some serious healing. My heart had been shattered into pieces, and I could not mend it on my own. The only way it could be mended was to seek out who made it in the first place. I was born with it and didn't know how it got into my body, but I knew someone created it, and whoever created it would be able to mend it. Just as my son cries out to me when he needs something or when he needs comfort, I cried out to the maker. I cried out to GOD!

I started praying and asked God to please take my pain away. I have always prayed every night before going to sleep, and it became so routine that every time my head hit my pillow I automatically started praying without realizing it. For some reason, this prayer that I prayed, begging to be healed and crying out loud to God felt very different. I was very vulnerable. I remember sitting on my bed, clutching a picture of my daughter very tightly on my chest, and crying to God uncontrollably. My body began to shake, and I started getting scared . . . as if I were having an out of body experience. I had to force myself to gain some control so that I could perform a mental check on myself. I started asking silly questions, such as my name, my address, my husband's name, and my son's name just to make sure I was sane. That's how insane I was, but after this out of body episode, I felt so relieved. I felt that a HUGE load had been taken off my shoulders. I looked at myself in the mirror and knew I would be all right. I was ready for good days and bad days, but I knew I would be just fine because now I knew that God was listening. This relief that I felt was so beautiful, so calm, and so tender and loving. It felt as if someone was holding me in their arms and saying, "Don't worry about a thing," and I was safe. I longed to feel more and more like this because I had never felt this good in my whole life. At this point, I felt way happier than I was even before the death of my daughter!

The Best Thanksgiving!

Thanksgiving makes us really think what we are really thankful for! I remember when I was five months pregnant and found out we were expecting a baby girl. My whole family was overjoyed, maybe a little too much! We all said how we will have a baby girl with us on Thanksgiving and couldn't wait for the day! A couple of months later God took our daughter to be one of his angels. The day we laid our baby girl to rest in walked my long lost friend at the funeral home. She walked up to the little casket and gave respect to my little girl. As she turned around, I noticed that she was pregnant! She came to my house, and I later found out that she was expecting a little girl one month after my baby was to have been born! I was so happy for her but yet nervous because of what had happened to me. We stayed in touch until she had a beautiful 10-lb. baby girl. I went to see her as soon as I could, and she asked if I could be the godmother of her baby. I was so touched. It felt that God was giving me a daughter right in front of me, and as I was sitting at my in-laws for Thanksgiving, I asked them if they remembered how we were all excited that we were going to have a baby girl among us on Thanksgiving, and we all had an "Aha!" moment. We were spending our Thanksgiving with a beautiful little baby girl. Baby Ella was lying peacefully among us! God had fulfilled our wishes.

God wasn't done with me that year. One of my girlfriends was expecting a baby girl the same day that my baby Clarette Belle was supposed to have been born. We had the same due date, and they were both girls, so we called them twins. We went through the whole pregnancy together, and when mine ended in tragedy, I tried my best to go through her pregnancy with her. My girlfriend was so devastated just as I had been. It was almost as if she had lost a baby too. I didn't know how I was going to handle the news that she had her baby. I was scared for her and excited at the same time. It was her first baby, but it would have been my second one. I wanted her to feel the joy of being a parent. When she had the baby, she sent me a picture, and I could see my daughter in her daughter's eyes. Zahra was such a beautiful baby. I loved her to pieces! My girlfriend asked me to be her baby's godmother. I humbly agreed. In one year, I gained two little daughters and an angel with our family name. How blessed was I? What great love I have from above!

Did my daughter leave us so that I could get the chance to taste this comfort . . . this level of happiness? The kind of happiness that takes virtually all the worry from your life and makes you feel that God supports you? Yes, my daughter was gone, but I was happy—happier than ever before! I would see tears of joy in my eyes day after day, night after night. I was broken into a new whole. I know the journey is not over, but I know God is behind me, and even through the loss of my beloved baby girl, I was and still am ridiculously happy! In fact, when I returned to work after my medical leave, a new employee looked at me and said, "Clementine, you are happy all the time. You must go to church all the time!" Can you believe it? No matter what I have gone through in life, I thank God for everything I have because He is the one who has provided it. I lost my daughter, but I have so many blessings that it's truly amazing. I thank Him for all these gifts He has blessed me with, and I know He has not finished taking care of me. He has my back. Like my son says in his nightly prayers, "Thank you God for Everything."

Shown below is a picture of a page from a memory book we created for baby Clarette Belle. Those socks are the socks that were put on her little feet when she was born. My son's hands are holding them with my hands at the bottom.

Some people believe in angels, I held one in my arms.

Breaking into a Whole

"Let us rejoice in our suffering, knowing that suffering produces endurance, endurance produces character, character produces hope, and hope does not disappoint us." (Romans 3:3-5). The breakdown we all experience in life leads us to break through.

Breaking strengthens you. As with lifting weights, we have to break our capillaries before we can build strength. For us to build emotional strength and endurance, we have to experience suffering. Through pain and healing, strength comes along. I see this all the time when a friend is going through tough times and feels that it is the end of the world and the pain will never end. My advice for them is to go through the pain and actually be excited because what they will turn out to be will be amazing. Their new amazing selves will develop out of the pain and struggle.

Breaking refines and frees you. Do not be afraid of crying throughout your pain. Crying is healthy and human. Tears are a great way to wash away the impurities of fear and attachment and clear the channels for love to freely flow. When I was crying out to God with my baby's picture in my hands, I let everything out. I let out all the struggles I had faced since I was a child. I felt that all the emotions that had been bottled up inside me were coming out. I shook as this transformation was happening. When I was done, I felt free. I felt lighter! I let go of all my fears and worries and agony and put them on the table and handed them all to God. I was tired of the load I had been carrying all these years—a load that no counseling, no pills, and no amount of alcohol or drugs would ever take away. When you are breaking, you need a permanent solution that will hold the new exciting you that you are about to become. I let go of it all and let God take over!

Breaking qualifies you. Thinking back at the hatred, bullying, beatings, and discrimination I have faced, I feel worthy and qualified to go through the toughest times that may be ahead of me. Nothing can shake me. I might as well create a "life experience" resume to clarify my qualifications and life experiences and hand it to the next tragic event that might hit me. As soon as it reads my resume, it will knock on the next door. I'm simply overqualified and you should be too. Armed with experience, appreciation of where suffering has led me as a person, and knowing that God is with me every step of the way, I believe I can achieve what I want to. If I had lived a pretty easy life of leisure, getting everything handed to me and sheltered from all the worldly struggles and pain, I doubt my perspective in life would be the way it is right now. Those that have led lives of relative comfort, ease, wealth, and physical gratification may not be as likely to question the nature of reality. Why should they when everything in the physical world goes their way? Painful experiences cause us to question our lives and reality. If we question often enough, we may realize that there is much more to us than our physical bodies and the physical world. This realization occurs because of tragic and trying experiences that cause us to question life. Looking at life through this perspective can help us to understand that painful experiences help us flourish.

When our lives are free from pain, it's easy to deceive ourselves, thinking we are invincible. It's only when the pressure of suffering comes that we are able to see who we really are—what we are really made of. I'm not saying you should go out and run into a raging fire so that you cannot experience pain and suffering in order to grow, and I'm not suggesting that you stab yourself and feel the pain to grow. What I'm saying, though, is that we can use the pain we have endured in the past to grow. We just need to make this a choice. Because of this experience, I'm grateful for all the suffering and breaking. I'm happily broken!

Breaking connects you to others. When pain is shared, it creates more meaning. It can create a movement. Look around you at those who have lost children or refugees who have gone through the same struggles or families with children with developmental disabilities. These experiences and challenges connect us. Our newfound relationships with others become deep, and some fall apart. When we look at others who have struggled, we can see ourselves in them and can easily identify with them. Even though I have never been to Asia or the Middle East, I feel connected to refugees from those countries. I do not speak their language, but our eyes speak to each other. I connect with them, and I'm able to provide the support I know they need.

I have created great relationships with people who have not had a similar past. Breaking not only connects you with similar people but also with people who have never led a life like yours. Because of our tragic life, we are all of a sudden "interesting" or "inspiring" or "authentic." How many of us want to be around interesting, inspiring, and authentic people? I do! Bringing a different perspective to someone's life can be the best thing one can do for another. One of my blog readers told me that she was leaving her job to start a new business she is passionate about because she read my blog. She wants to live life fully. She doesn't want to waste any more time. Despite past challenges, she believed enough is enough and that her time had come! Life happens for us, so in every hurtful and challenging situation, try to take advantage of that moment and flourish with better and healthier behaviors. This pain and suffering that used to cause us discomfort help us understand ourselves better. We become self-assured, authentic, strong, unshakable, and we develop a newfound faith, connectedness, and resilience.

Happily Broken

I'm grateful for my brokenness. Allowing myself to break and be transformed has and still is transforming me into a better, happier person every day. I know that the pain I have endured in the past has made it possible for me to experience my essential nature. I got to know myself at a deeper level. Even though it was scary, it was freeing at the same time.

I have also realized that breaking is very crucial for my happiness. It's easier to love and understand others since I have been broken. I appreciate the house I live in because I once lived in refugee camps. I appreciate every meal because I was once hungry. I appreciate my relationships with others because I was once treated as an outcast. I appreciate the peace I feel when I think of Jesus because His place in my heart wasn't as visible as it is now. I'm so happy that I have been blessed with all that I have. Every morning when I wake up I smile because I know I'm a masterpiece. It's a wonderful world we live in. I would not change anything about my past experiences, and I welcome future ones. I love and appreciate every breath I take. Until I stop breathing, my mission is to share my wholeness with my fellow brothers and sisters. This means you!

Many Thanks to:

The University of Dayton

Fallon Health Employees

Lifesong Church

UMass Memorial Hospital

Lee Snead

My family and friends

My readers

More on Me

✓ I love dancing. Beyonce's music does something to me.

✓ Every New Year I am concerned that I will dance too much and dislocate my knees. This anxiety is real because it has happened a couple of times. My husband has banned me from dancing "Gangnam Style" because it hurt me. I spent one New Year's in an emergency room!

✓ I would like to meet Oprah one day. Nelson Mandela was on the list, but he left before I could meet him.

✓ My dream home is a house that reminds me of my parents' house in Rwanda. I left too soon and never got to enjoy it.

Need a Speaker or a Workshop Leader?

As an inspirational guest speaker, my mission is to connect with my audience on a personal level. I encourage my listeners to travel to my past and come back to their present with an enhanced process of thinking—one that will open their eyes and hearts to the glorious life that we so often take for granted. Every human being is blessed with the ability to pursue a life of happiness and success, and when audience members walk away with this understanding and inspiration to change, I know I have done my job.

I'm available to conduct keynotes, workshops, and training sessions on various topics, including the following:

The Terrifying Beauty of Pain
Agony and sorrow can lead you to wisdom and eventual happiness if you attempt to recognize the process. Painful experiences build onto our character and experiential intelligence, allowing us to advance in humanity. This presentation is dedicated to understanding the process of pain and

suffering and how they enhance personal and spiritual growth. You will learn how to use your pain and brokenness to your advantage.

When Giving Up is Not an Option

As human beings, we tend to give up too easily. We give up on our dreams, jobs, relationships, and health because someone says NO to us or because we have failed once and take it as a sign that it's not meant to be. I started facing rejection at a very young age as a refugee. When I was eight years old, I had to fend for myself when my parents disappeared for two weeks. We lived in refugee camps, where we faced death right in the eyes every day. When I used a "log" as an anchor to swim toward a shirt in Lake Kivu and finally realized it was actually a dead body of a fellow Rwandan, I felt that life was not worth living. When I got to the USA and was bullied every day in high school for being "different," I would want to quit school. In my adult life, I lost a daughter when I was 27 weeks pregnant. This was my breaking point, but I had to be resilient—resilient for my young son, resilient for my family, resilient for my country, and resilient for the world. This talk will leave the audience feeling resilient, renewed, and ready to fight to WIN in their businesses, their relationships, and their health—anything that affects them.

Antibullying

Schools across America are plagued with the deadly disease of bullying. Of all my challenges, discrimination from peers continues to be one of the most terrifying I've had to endure. It is imperative that schools take immediate action to tackle bullying and find a solution to this growing problem. This talk will focus on the importance of diversity, appreciating the uniqueness of others, and how to overcome being bullied.

Your Mark in the World Starts NOW

Empowered students represent our future. This talk empowers students to not only be strong and inspiring leaders but to also be authentic. This talk will leave them feeling that they are true masterpieces. They will see their struggles, whether educational or personal, as tools to elevate them to where they want to be—at the top. They will learn that understanding people and using their unique talents will help them be better leaders. They will understand that LIFE happens FOR you and not AGAINST you. I'm able to personalize talks for most audiences.

Satisfied Customers

"We just held our second Diversity Week at Bartlett, and we had a phenomenal speaker come, Clementine Bihiga. She is a Rwandan genocide survivor and published author of *Happily Broken*. The students are still talking about her, and we have an order of her books coming to the school that the students bought. She has a really powerful message about bullying, about not giving up hope, and about being happy. The entire auditorium was silent when she spoke except when she made them laugh (she has a great sense of humor), and she received a standing ovation from the student body." — Barlett Junior High School

"Clementine Bihiga is a truly remarkable woman. She came to speak to the women in my HOPE for Women Program at a luncheon. When Clementine speaks, her voice is filled with joy, even as she tells the audience the horrific stories and experiences she has endured throughout her life. Her unique sense of telling her story and the way she always found the silver lining in everything is amazing. Clementine changes lives in such a positive way. She speaks and people listen. She allows her audience to be themselves. Through humor and strength, she taught us all that we can say, 'I Got This.' Even through tough times we can be happy. Her compassion and positive energy is truly a gift.I would most definitely

recommend any company or organization looking for a motivational, inspiring, funny, and energetic speaker to call on Clementine Bihiga to speak. She is remarkable. She will exceed your expectations."
— Allyson C., HOPE For Women.

"I cannot begin to find the words that can explain the gratitude I feel toward Clementine for speaking at our school. The message was incredibly powerful and has stuck with our kids. She not only shared her story but promoted the ideal of hope and loving yourself and being happy. Our students were engaged throughout the entire presentation. You could hear a pin drop except when she made them laugh (her humor is contagious). She received a standing ovation from our students (who can sometimes be a skeptical crowd). Students lined up afterwards to meet her and purchase her book. We have purchased two copies for a school library, a class set, and many of our teachers are just reading it with their classes. She is eloquent, beautiful, and relevant. We were blessed to have her speak at our school and hope to bring her back again to our Diversity Week next year. I would highly recommend her to speak at any function." — Sarah A., Barlett Junior High School

"Clementine recently spoke at a luncheon of around 20 women in attendance. Right away, she was so inviting and charismatic as she told her unimaginable childhood story. No bitterness, just positive energy filled the room, making the event intimate and inspiring. Clementine is absolutely worthy of speaking engagements that uplift and celebrate gratitude, especially for the female population." — Kathy B.

"I interviewed Clementine for THE IMMIGRANT ENTREPRENEUR podcast. I was extremely impressed by her confidence, humility, authentic character, and sincerity. She also manifested a great spectrum of knowledge, experience, and compassion in her area of expertise." —
Kent T., Immigrant Entrepreneur

I would love to hear from you. Please visit my website at www.clementinebihiga.com or email me at info@clementinebihiga.com

Please remember to rate my book on Amazon.com. This helps me deliver what my readers want. I also want to know your honest opinion. I really appreciate your help.

Made in the USA
Middletown, DE
17 March 2016